Jumbo Book of
Toddler Fun

This book belongs to...

_____

Editor: Liza Charlesworth
Cover design: Tannaz Fassihi
Cover art: Kevin Zimmer
Interior design: Mina Chen
Interior illustrations: 141,155,157-159, 299 (John Lund), 214,215, 217, 219, 231, 236-261(Doug Jones), 301, 313 (Jannie Ho)
All other images: Shutterstock.com

ISBN 978-1-338-89107-2
Scholastic Inc., 557 Broadway, New York, NY 10012
Copyright © 2023 Scholastic Inc.
All rights reserved. Printed in the U.S.A.
First printing, January 2023

1 2 3 4 5 6 7 8 9 10   144   32 31 30 29 28 27 26 25 24 23

Dear Parent,

Congratulations! You've chosen the perfect resource for your joyful, creative, curious toddler! At Scholastic we know it is never too early to get started on a journey of learning—especially when that journey is customized for very young children AND is super fun!

Toward that end, this colorful workbook is jam-packed with age-perfect activities related to tracing, coloring, drawing, cutting and pasting, matching, sorting, alphabet, numbers, and shapes.

We've also included interactive rhymes and songs to boost language development and pre-reading skills. In addition, you'll find bonus activities for you and your child to complete together PLUS bright stickers to celebrate their BIG gains in learning.

And here's more good news: We provided two sections related to each topic—the second slightly more challenging than the first—to ensure your child gets plenty of playful, confidence-boosting practice.

So, turn the page and get started today! This workbook, created by the educational experts at Scholastic, will help set your toddler on the path to a lifetime of exciting learning.

Learning Is a Joy With the
Jumbo Book of Toddler Fun!

The toddler years are an exciting time to play and learn. This workbook has been carefully designed to maximize the fun as your child acquires important skills. On the pages that follow, you'll find 250+ age-perfect activities in 10 topic areas.

Tracing
(pages 9–18 & 162–170)

Coloring
(pages 19–30 & 171–182)

Drawing
(pages 31–39 & 183–191)

Cutting & Pasting
(pages 40–60 & 192–212)

Matching
(pages 61–69 & 213–221)

Sorting
(pages 70–82 & 222–234)

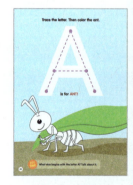

Alphabet
(pages 83–110 & 235–262)

Numbers
(pages 111–122 & 263–274)

Shapes
(pages 123–132 & 275–284)

Interactive Rhymes & Songs
(pages 133–161 & 285–314)

About the Activity Pages

It is likely that your exuberant toddler keeps you VERY busy. For that reason, we've made this workbook VERY simple. Each activity requires just a few supplies (see page 6) and absolutely no prep. Here's a quick tour of one page.

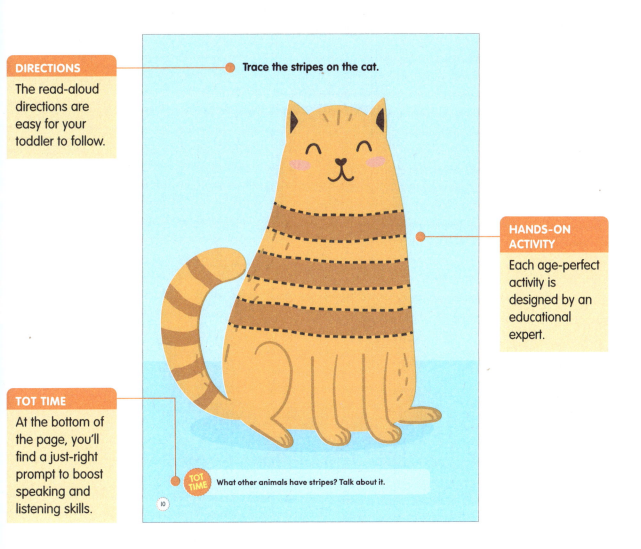

DIRECTIONS
The read-aloud directions are easy for your toddler to follow.

Trace the stripes on the cat.

HANDS-ON ACTIVITY
Each age-perfect activity is designed by an educational expert.

TOT TIME
At the bottom of the page, you'll find a just-right prompt to boost speaking and listening skills.

TOT TIME What other animals have stripes? Talk about it.

IO

But wait. There's more. This very special workbook also includes…

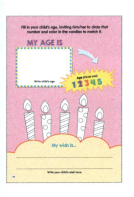

BONUS ACTIVITIES
Both you and your little one will love these fill-in pages to celebrate his or her special personality and talents.

STICKER SHEET
Motivate your toddler to learn and reward hard work with these big, bright stickers.

Quick Tips to Maximize Learning and Fun

Welcome to the *Jumbo Book of Toddler Fun*! Here are some quick ideas to ensure your child's learning experience is stress-free, safe, and fun.

GATHER SIMPLE SUPPLIES

It's a good idea to gather the necessary tools your toddler will need BEFORE the learning journey begins. Don't worry, we've kept things VERY simple.

Nontoxic Crayons: To complete the workbook pages, these 10 colors are required: red, blue, yellow, green, orange, purple, pink, brown, black, and white. Consider purchasing large-size or special toddler-grip crayons to accommodate your child's small hands. (Washable markers can also be used, but will require close supervision.)

Safety Scissors: The cut-and-paste sections of this workbook require a pair of small safety scissors. We suggest plastic ones, which are available at most office supply stores. Remember to always supervise children when using scissors.

Nontoxic Glue Stick: Your child will also need a glue stick. A large size is preferable, as it is easier for small hands to grip and manipulate.

STORAGE TIP: We suggest you keep these tools in a plastic bin stored beside the workbook. That way, your toddler will be able to sit down and learn—in an instant.

SAFETY FIRST!

TODDLERS ARE INQUISITIVE AND CURIOUS. That makes them prone to put things in their mouths, such as crayons or glue sticks. In addition, they lack fine motor skills, which can cause even safety scissors to be slightly hazardous. For that reason, make sure to explain and model the safe use of these items. And if your toddler is too young to understand, simply put the workbook and tools away for a few months until he or she is ready to use them.

MOST IMPORTANT, MAKE SURE TO NEVER LEAVE YOUR TODDLER UNSUPERVISED—EVEN WITH A WORKBOOK AND CRAYONS. TWO- AND THREE-YEAR-OLDS ARE UNPREDICTABLE, AND THEIR SAFETY SHOULD ALWAYS BE YOUR FIRST PRIORITY.

Set the Stage for Learning

• **Invite your toddler to dip into this workbook a few times a week or more, but be sure to keep it a joyful experience.** Turn to the pages when he or she is alert, focused, and ready to learn. If your child is frustrated or cranky, go to the playground or read a toddler-perfect book. We've included a list of some favorites on the following page.

• **Choose a quiet, comfy, clutter-free location to learn.** A tabletop, high chair, or the floor are great options. Make sure you can see and supervise your child at all times.

• **Read the directions aloud to your toddler, then complete the pages together.** At first, your child may need a lot of guidance and help. That said, as he or she grows accustomed to the activities, your toddler will probably be able to complete many of the pages independently.

• **Set reasonable expectations for your toddler.** For example, your child may color wildly outside the lines, have a hard time tracing a number 3, or need your steady hand to help cut and paste a circle. No worries! It is a triumph for young children to sit, focus, and simply try. It is also a triumph for them to enjoy acquiring new skills. Feeling free to take risks and make mistakes is a big part of the early learning process. If your toddler colors a ladybug green instead of red, applaud his or her effort. Why? Every time children use a crayon, they learn about colors. Every time children point to a letter *T*, they develop alphabet skills. Every time children trace a star or cut out a square, they build important fine motor skills.

• **Remember, each child gains mastery at a different pace.** At age two or three, toddlers are at the very beginning of their learning journey. They will have many years to hone their coloring, writing, counting, reading, and cutting skills. So, relax and enjoy. The most important thing is that your child feels good about trying new things. For that reason, it's a great idea to follow up a learning session with a happy thumbs-up or a reward sticker. Sending the message that attaining knowledge is an enjoyable experience is one of the greatest gifts you can give your toddler.

Terrific Books for Toddlers

Looking for some engaging read-alouds for your little learner? Choose books with simple plots, playful language, and colorful illustrations or photos. Here are a few of our very favorite titles.

Kiss, Kiss, Little Fish
by Sandra Magsamen
(Scholastic)

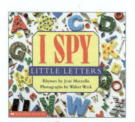

I Spy Little Letters
by Jean Marzollo
(Scholastic)

Dream Big, Little One by Vashti
Harrison (Scholastic)

Big Feelings
by Alexandra Penfold
(Scholastic)

Arroz Con Leche: Popular Songs and Rhymes from Latin America selected by
Lulu Delacre (Scholastic)

I Am a Garbage Truck
by Ace Landers
(Scholastic)

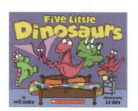

Five Little Dinosaurs
by Will Grace
(Scholastic)

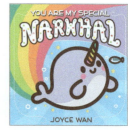

You Are My Very Special Narwhal
by Joyce Wan
(Scholastic)

Peppa's Chinese New Year
(Scholastic)

Sweet, Sweet Baby
by Javaka Steptoe
(Scholastic)

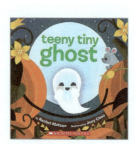

Teeny Tiny Ghost
by Rachel Matson
(Scholastic)

Goodnight, Butterfly
by Ross Burach
(Scholastic)

TRACING

SUPPLIES: crayons or washable markers

The pages in this section provide a wide range of easy tracing activities. Not only is tracing enjoyable, it's a great way to lay the foundation for drawing and writing success. Simply read the directions aloud, then invite your toddler to trace the lines, waves, spots, and shapes.

If your child struggles to trace the dashed images, feel free to guide his or her hand. Over time and with practice, you'll likely see greater accuracy. For now, focus on fostering a love of trying new things—from tracing to coloring to writing and beyond!

Follow up your child's coloring sessions with the TOT TIME activities at the bottom of the page. These fun prompts will help build early speaking and listening skills.

Trace the stripes on the cat.

 TOT TIME What other animals have stripes? Talk about it.

Trace the spots on the dog.

 What other animals have spots? Talk about it.

11

Trace the bear's bubbles.

TOT TIME Blow some bubbles with your child, then talk about them!

Trace the stripes on the gift box.

For You!

 TOT TIME Invite your child to imagine what is inside the box.

13

Trace the spaghetti in the monster's bowl.

 TOT TIME This monster loves spaghetti! What is your child's favorite food?

Trace the penguin's ice cream scoops.

TOT TIME What is your child's favorite flavor of ice cream?
What is yours? Talk about it.

Trace each caterpillar's path to the leaf.

TOT TIME Talk about how caterpillars turn into butterflies when they "grow up."

Trace each butterfly's path to the flower.

Trace the rays of the sun.

TOT TIME Talk about the sun. Where and when do we see it?

COLORING

SUPPLIES: crayons or washable markers

The pages in this section will introduce your toddler to the colors red, blue, yellow, green, orange, purple, pink, brown, black, and white. Simply read the directions aloud, then invite your child to color each critter the appropriate color.

To maximize learning, point to the featured animal, such as the blue whale, and encourage your child to tell you about it. Then, take the opportunity to share a few simple fact facts, such as: *Blue whales live in the ocean. They are huge. They can wave their tails.*

Follow up your child's coloring sessions with the TOT TIME activities at the bottom of the page. These fun prompts will help build early speaking and listening skills.

Color the ladybug  red.

 TOT TIME Talk about other animals and objects that are red.

Color the whale  blue.

Talk about other animals and objects that are blue.

Color the chick  yellow.

 TOT TIME Talk about other animals and objects that are yellow.

Color the snake green.

 Talk about other animals and objects that are green.

Color the tiger  orange.

 TOT TIME **Talk about other animals and objects that are orange.**

Color the butterfly purple.

 TOT TIME Talk about other animals and objects that are purple.

Color the flamingo 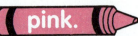 pink.

 Talk about other animals and objects that are pink.

Color the bear  brown.

 TOT TIME Talk about other animals and objects that are brown.

Color the bat black.

Talk about other animals and objects that are black.

Color the bunny white.

 TOT TIME Talk about other animals and objects that are white.

29

Color the fish rainbow.

 TOT TIME **Talk about other animals and objects that are many colors.**

DRAWING

SUPPLIES: crayons or washable markers

The pages in this section are designed to help your toddler develop early drawing skills. Simply read the directions aloud, then invite him or her to create stripes, spots, swirls, noodles, and more!

Remember, toddlers are just learning how to use crayons or markers, so don't worry if their attempts to draw straight stripes look more like wiggly worms. The goal is for them to enjoy the experience and gain dexterity over time.

Follow up your child's drawing sessions with the TOT TIME activities at the bottom of the page. These fun prompts will help build early speaking and listening skills.

Draw more curly hair on the monster.

Name this monster and make up a story about it.

Draw more straight hair on the monster.

Name this monster and make up a story about it.

Draw more noodles for the poodle.

 TOT TIME *Poodle* rhymes with *noodle*. Share more rhyming words with your child.

Draw more bubbles in the dinosaur's tub.

Treat your toddler to a bubble bath. What words describe bubbles?

Draw more wiggly worms in the garden.

TOT TIME What living things does your child see in this garden?

Draw more waves in the ocean.

TOT TIME What living things does your child see in this ocean?

37

Draw a happy face and a sad face.

What makes your child happy and sad? Talk about it.

Draw a scoop of ice cream on each cone.

 Is ice cream hot or cold? Sweet or sour? Talk about it.

CUTTING & PASTING

SUPPLIES: safety scissors and nontoxic glue stick

The pages in this section are designed to introduce your toddler to cutting and pasting, which will build important fine motor skills. Simply read the directions aloud, then work together to cut and paste the shapes to create surprise pictures. NOTE: Always supervise children when using scissors.

If your toddler is too young to cut out a shape effectively, feel free to guide his or her hand when using the safety scissors. Or, do the cutting yourself. The gluing, too, can be done with or without your help. Cutting and pasting are skills that takes time and practice, so be patient and focus on fun.

Follow up your child's cutting-and-pasting sessions with the TOT TIME activities at the bottom of the page. These fun prompts will help build early speaking and listening skills.

Cut out the circle and paste it on page 43.

Paste the circle here. What do you see?

 TOT TIME Talk about the sun. Can you think of some words to describe it?

Talk about this sunny day. What do you see?

TOT TIME What does your child like to do on a sunny day? Talk about it.

Cut out the square and paste it on page 47.

Paste the square here. What do you see?

TOT TIME Who lives in this house? Talk about it.

Talk about this apartment building.
What animals live here?

TOT TIME Make up a silly story about one—or all—of the animals that live in this building.

Cut out the triangle and paste it on page 51.

Paste the triangle here. What do you see?

51

TOT TIME Along with your child, sing "Happy Birthday" to this bear cub.

How old is this bear cub? What do you see at his party?

TOT TIME What did this bear cub wish for when he blew out the candles? Make up a story about it!

Cut out the rectangle and paste it on page 55.

Paste the rectangle here. What do you see?

TOT TIME A tree is a home for animals. What animals does your child see?

Talk about this owl. What does it say?

Hoot!

TOT TIME Owls say "HOOT!" What sounds do other animals make?

Cut out the oval and paste it on page 59.

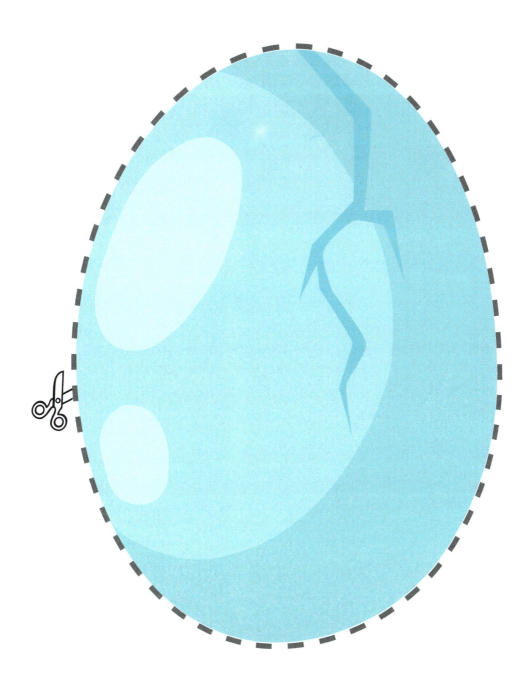

Paste the oval here. What do you see?

TOT TIME What is inside the egg? Invite your child to guess.

Talk about the nest and hatched egg. What do you see?

TOT TIME Talk about other animals that hatch from eggs, including owls, frogs, and fish.

MATCHING

SUPPLIES: crayons or washable markers

The pages in this section are designed to introduce your toddler to the important concept of one-to-one correspondence, otherwise known as *matching*. Simply read the directions, then invite him or her to draw lines to make matches. NOTE: A dashed line is provided for the first match.

If your child struggles to draw straight lines, feel free to guide his or her hand. Remember, the primary goal is to practice and build dexterity over time. To boost early vocabulary skills, challenge your child to point to each pair of pictured items, such as *fish*, and say their name.

Follow up your child's matching sessions with the TOT TIME activities at the bottom of the page. These fun prompts will help build early speaking and listening skills.

Draw lines to match the pets.

Draw lines to match the toys.

Draw lines to match the fruits.

 Challenge your child to name these fruits.
Discuss other kinds of fruits.

Draw lines to match the things that go.

Challenge your child to name these things that go.
Discuss other kinds of vehicles.

Draw lines to match the small animals.

Draw lines to match the big animals.

 Challenge your child to name these large animals.
Discuss other kinds of large animals.

67

Draw lines to match the treats.

 Challenge your child to name these treats.
Discuss other kinds of treats.

Draw lines to match the workbook tools.

 TOT TIME Challenge your child to name these workbook tools. Discuss other kinds of workbook tools.

69

SORTING

SUPPLIES: safety scissors, nontoxic glue stick

The pages in this section introduce toddlers to sorting AND reinforce cutting-and-pasting skills. Simply read the directions, then invite your child to cut out the two animals at the bottom of the page and paste each in the correct group. NOTE: Always supervise children when using scissors.

If your toddler is too young to cut effectively, feel free to guide his or her hand when using the safety scissors. The gluing, too, can be done with or without your help. Cutting and pasting are skills that take time and practice, so be patient and focus on fun.

Follow up your child's sorting sessions with the TOT TIME activities at the bottom of the page. These instant prompts will help build early speaking and listening skills.

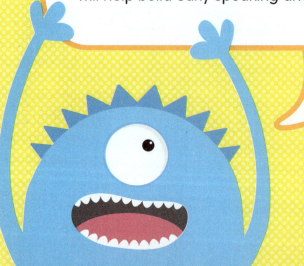

**Cut out the pets at the bottom of the page.
Then, paste each in the right group.**

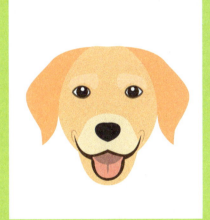

Talk to your toddler about how cats and dogs are alike and different.

Cut out the farm animals at the bottom of the page. Then, paste each in the right group.

Talk to your toddler about how cows and horses are alike and different.

Pretend to be a cow, then a horse.
Challenge your toddler to copy you.

Cut out the insects at the bottom of the page.
Then, paste each in the right group.

TOT TIME Talk to your toddler about how butterflies and bees are alike and different.

Pretend to be a butterfly, then a bee.
Challenge your toddler to copy you.

Cut out the birds at the bottom of the page. Then, paste each in the right group.

TOT TIME

Talk to your toddler about how penguins and ducks are alike and different.

Pretend to be a penguin, then a duck.
Challenge your toddler to copy you.

Cut out the small animals at the bottom of the page. Then, paste each in the right group.

TOT TIME

Talk to your toddler about how frogs and mice are alike and different.

Pretend to be a frog, then a mouse.
Challenge your toddler to copy you.

Cut out the jungle animals at the bottom of the page. Then, paste each in the right group.

TOT TIME

Talk to your toddler about how lions and elephants are alike and different.

Pretend to be an elephant, then a lion.
Challenge your toddler to copy you.

ALPHABET

SUPPLIES: crayons or washable markers

The pages in this section will introduce your toddler to the awesome letters *A* through *Z*! Simply read the directions aloud, then invite him or her to trace the featured letter, such as *A*, and color the animal that begins with it, such as *ant*.

For added enjoyment, have a simple conversation about the featured animal. What does your child know about ants? What information can you share to help him or her learn more about these incredible creatures?

Follow up your child's alphabet sessions with the TOT TIME activities at the bottom of the page. These fun prompts will help build early speaking and listening skills.

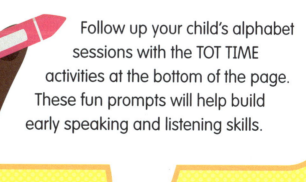

Trace the letter. Then color the ant.

is for ANT!

 TOT TIME — What else begins with the letter A? Talk about it.

Trace the letter. Then color the bear.

is for **BEAR!**

TOT TIME What else begins with the letter B? Talk about it.

Trace the letter. Then color the cat.

is for **CAT!**

 TOT TIME What else begins with the letter C? Talk about it.

Trace the letter. Then color the dog.

is for **DOG!**

 TOT TIME What else begins with the letter D? Talk about it.

87

Trace the letter. Then color the elephant.

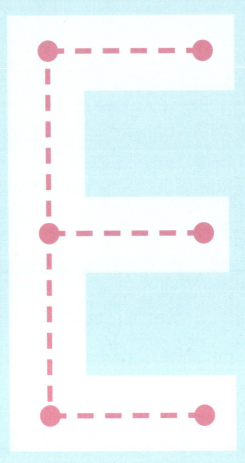

is for **ELEPHANT!**

TOT TIME What else begins with the letter E? Talk about it.

Trace the letter. Then color the fox.

is for **FOX!**

TOT TIME What else begins with the letter F? Talk about it.

Trace the letter. Then color the gorilla.

is for **GORILLA!**

 TOT TIME What else begins with the letter G? Talk about it.

Trace the letter. Then color the horse.

is for **HORSE!**

TOT TIME What else begins with the letter H? Talk about it.

Trace the letter. Then color the iguana.

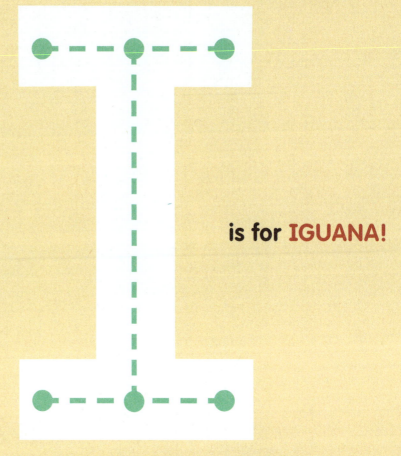

is for IGUANA!

 TOT TIME What else begins with the letter I? Talk about it.

Trace the letter. Then color the jaguar.

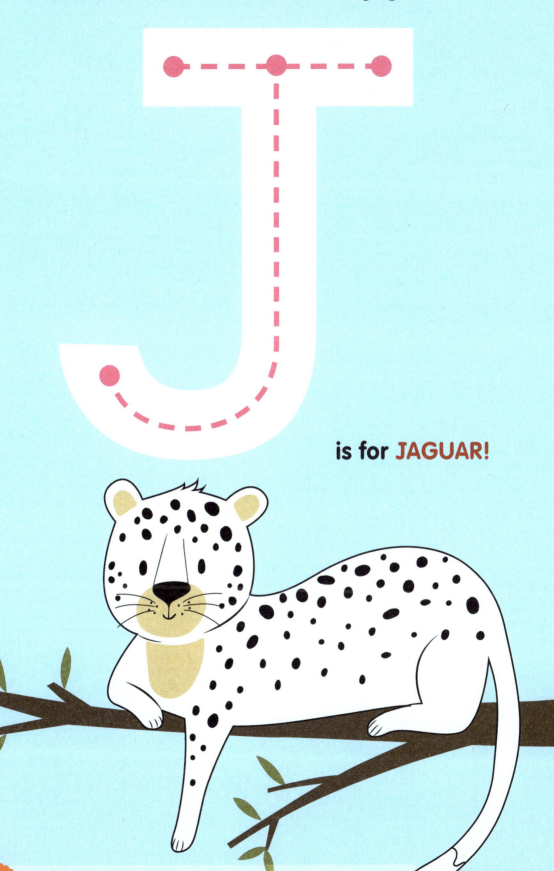

is for JAGUAR!

TOT TIME What else begins with the letter J? Talk about it.

Trace the letter. Then color the kangaroo.

K

is for KANGAROO!

TOT TIME What else begins with the letter K? Talk about it.

Trace the letter. Then color the lion.

L is for **LION!**

TOT TIME What else begins with the letter L? Talk about it.

95

Trace the letter. Then color the mouse.

is for **MOUSE!**

 TOT TIME What else begins with the letter M? Talk about it.

Trace the letter. Then color the nest.

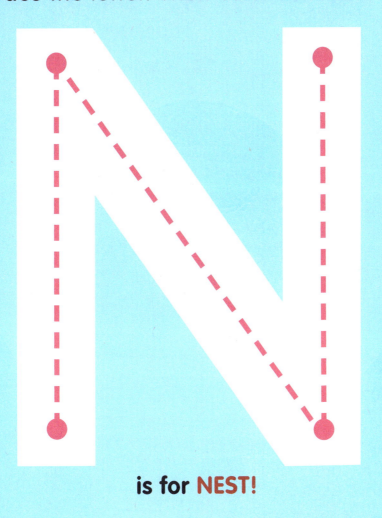

is for **NEST!**

TOT TIME What else begins with the letter N? Talk about it.

Trace the letter. Then color the octopus.

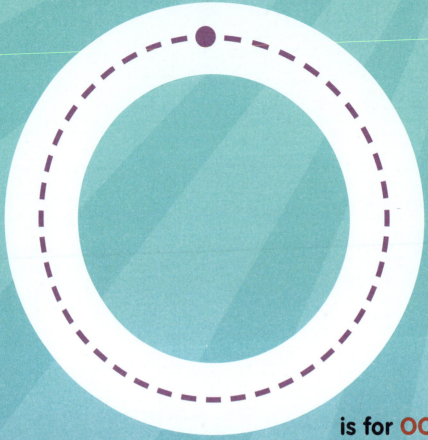

is for OCTOPUS!

TOT TIME What else begins with the letter O? Talk about it.

Trace the letter. Then color the pig.

P is for **PIG!**

Trace the letter. Then color the quail.

Q

is for **QUAIL!**

TOT TIME What else begins with the letter Q? Talk about it.

Trace the letter. Then color the rabbit.

is for RABBIT!

 TOT TIME What else begins with the letter R? Talk about it.

Trace the letter. Then color the seal.

is for **SEAL!**

Trace the letter. Then color the tiger.

is for **TIGER!**

 TOT TIME What else begins with the letter T? Talk about it.

Trace the letter. Then color the umbrellabird.

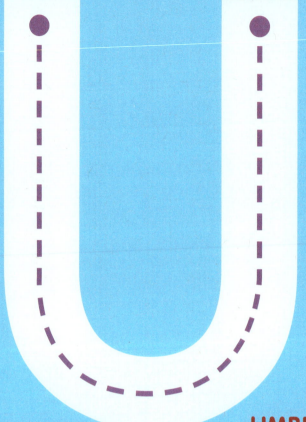

is for
UMBRELLABIRD!

 TOT TIME What else begins with the letter U? Talk about it.

Trace the letter. Then color the velociraptor.

is for **VELOCIRAPTOR!**

TOT TIME   What else begins with the letter V? Talk about it.

105

Trace the letter. Then color the warthog.

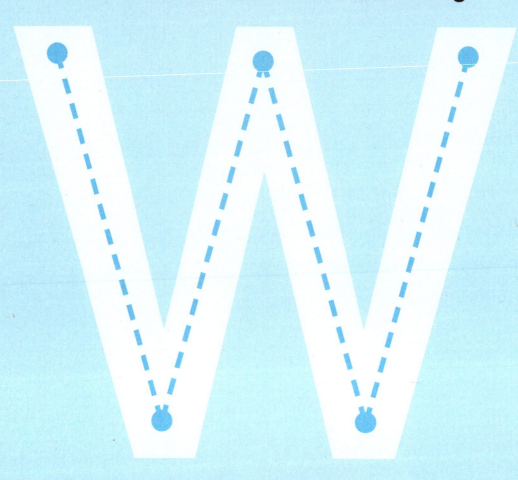

is for **WARTHOG!**

TOT TIME What else begins with the letter W? Talk about it.

Trace the letter. Then color the X-Ray fish.

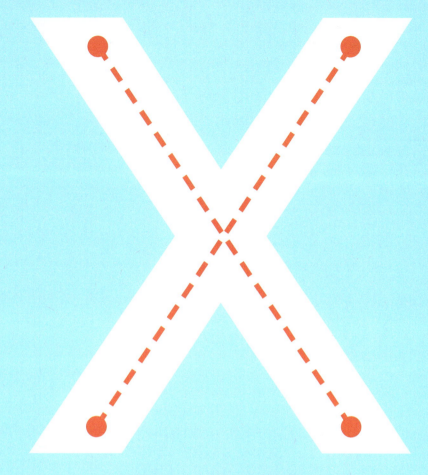

is for **X-RAY FISH!**

TOT TIME What else begins with the letter X? Talk about it.

107

Trace the letter. Then color the yak.

is for **YAK!**

 TOT TIME What else begins with the letter Y? Talk about it.

Trace the letter. Then color the zebra.

Z is for ZEBRA!

TOT TIME What else begins with the letter Z? Talk about it.

109

Color the alphabet quilt.

	A	B	C
D	E	F	G
H	I	J	K
L	M	N	O
P	Q	R	S
T	U	V	W
X	Y	Z	

TOT TIME Point to each letter, saying its name with your child.

NUMBERS

SUPPLIES: crayons or washable markers

The pages in this section will introduce your toddler to the terrific numbers I through 10! Simply read the directions aloud, then invite him or her to trace the featured number, such as *I*, and color the corresponding picture: *one car*.

To reinforce early number sense, work with your child to count the items on each page, such as *one car*, *two planes*, or *three teddy bears*.

Follow up your child's number sessions with the TOT TIME activities at the bottom of the page. These fun prompts will help build early speaking and listening skills.

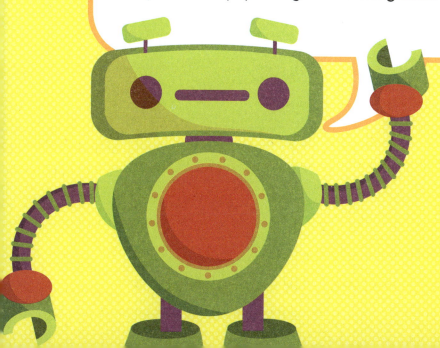

Trace the number. Then color the car.

TOT TIME Invite your child to finish this sentence: There is 1 _____.

Trace the number. Then color the airplanes.

TOT TIME

Invite your child to finish this sentence: There are 2 _____.

113

Trace the number. Then color the teddy bears.

TOT TIME Invite your child to finish this sentence: There are 3 _____.

Trace the number. Then color the dolls.

Invite your child to finish this sentence: There are 4 _____.

Trace the number. Then color the kites.

TOT TIME Invite your child to finish this sentence: There are 5 _____.

Trace the number. Then color the balls.

TOT TIME Invite your child to finish this sentence: There are 6 _____ .

Trace the number. Then color the books.

 TOT TIME Invite your child to finish this sentence: There are 7 _____.

Trace the number. Then color the cupcakes.

TOT TIME

Invite your child to finish this sentence: There are 8 _____.

119

Trace the number. Then color the hats.

Invite your child to finish this sentence: There are 9 _____.

120

Trace the number. Then color the balloons.

TOT TIME

Invite your child to finish this sentence: There are 10 _____.

121

Color the number blocks.

 TOT TIME Point to each number, saying its name with your child.

SHAPES

SUPPLIES: crayons or washable markers

The pages in this section will introduce your toddler to eight great shapes: triangles, squares, circles, rectangles, ovals, rhombuses, stars, and hearts. Simply read the directions aloud, then invite him or her to trace around the shapes.

To maximize learning, point to each pictured item, such as the pizza slice, and announce its shape: *triangle*. Then, talk about other items of the same shape.

Follow up your child's shape sessions with the TOT TIME activities at the bottom of the page. These fun prompts will help build early speaking and listening skills.

Trace the triangle shapes.

TOT TIME Invite your child to point to each picture and say its name with or without your help.

Trace the square shapes.

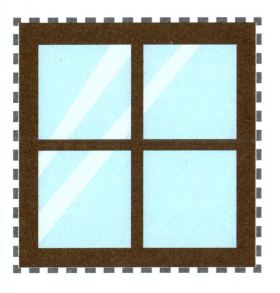

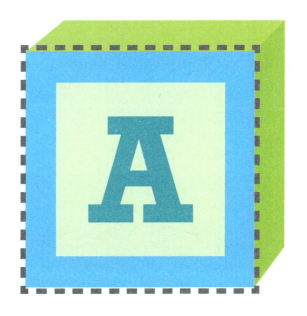

Trace the circle shapes.

TOT TIME Invite your child to point to each picture and say its name with or without your help.

Trace the rectangle shapes.

Toddler Tiger

 TOT TIME Invite your child to point to each picture and say its name with or without your help.

127

Trace the oval shapes.

Trace the rhombus shapes.

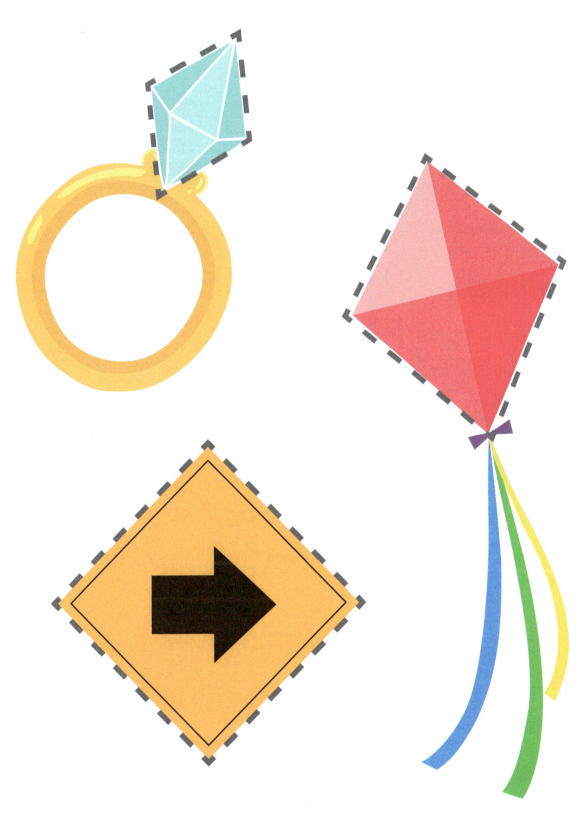

Invite your child to point to each picture and say its name with or without your help.

Trace the star shapes.

 TOT TIME Invite your child to point to each picture and say its name with or without your help.

Trace the heart shapes.

HUG ME

TOT TIME
Invite your child to point to each picture and say its name with or without your help.

131

Review and trace the shapes.

Invite your child to point to each picture and say its shape with or without your help.

EASY RHYMES

SUPPLIES: crayons or washable markers

Nursery rhymes are playful and packed with learning! Inviting your toddler to chant along to "Humpty Dumpty" or "Little Miss Muffet" boosts early speaking AND vocabulary skills. In addition, these "sticky" rhymes help children begin to understand the way that words work, setting the stage for reading success.

Read each rhyme slowly, clearly, and with verve—encouraging your toddler to join in. There is no such thing as repeating a rhyme too many times!

Don't forget to try the TOT TIME ideas at the bottom of the pages. These simple kinesthetic activities give kids the opportunity to jump, wiggle, dance, and do fingerplays. Last but not least, extend learning with each rhyme's companion page, which provide added opportunities to think, write, and draw.

Humpty Dumpty

Humpty Dumpty

sat on a wall.

Humpty Dumpty

had a great fall.

All the king's horses

and all the king's men

couldn't put Humpty

together again.

TOT TIME

On *Humpty Dumpty sat on a wall,* fold your arms to make a wall. On *had a great fall,* roll your arms. On *all the king's horses,* hold pretend horse reins. On *couldn't put Humpty together again,* shake your head *no.* Invite your toddler to copy you.

Help Humpty by putting a  on each of his broken parts.

TOT TIME Talk about ways your toddler can help a friend feel better, such as by offering a Band-Aid or a hug.

135

Peek-a-Boo

Peek-a-boo!

Peek-a-boo!

_____ sees me.
toddler's name

I see _____, too!
toddler's name

TOT TIME **Play peekaboo with your toddler as you read the rhyme.**

Trace the stripes on the T-shirt.

TOT TIME Invite your toddler to play peekaboo with a favorite stuffed toy. For example, hold a teddy bear in front of your face and say: *Peek-a-boo! Peek-a-boo! Leo sees Teddy. Teddy sees Leo, too!*

Pat-a-Cake

Pat-a-cake, pat-a-cake,

baker's man.

Bake me a cake as fast

as you can.

Pat it and prick it and

mark it with a *B*.

Put it in the oven

for baby and me.

 TOT TIME As you say the rhyme, have your toddler clap his/her hands, then clap yours. As he/she becomes more adept, add more hand motions, such as patting the dough or marking the cake with a *B*.

Trace the B and color it 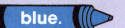 blue.

B is for *Baby*. Talk about other words that begin with *B*.

Say the rhyme with your toddler.

Hickory, Dickory, Dock

Hickory, dickory, dock,

the mouse ran up the clock.

The clock struck one,

the mouse ran down—

hickory, dickory, dock.

 On *the mouse ran up the clock*, run your fingers up your toddler's arm. On *the clock struck one*, clap. On *the mouse ran down*, run your fingers down your toddler's arm.

Color the mouse  brown.

 TOT TIME Talk about mice with your toddler. Ask: *What other animals are small?*

Teddy Bear, Teddy Bear

Teddy bear, teddy bear,

turn around!

Teddy bear, teddy bear,

touch the ground!

Teddy bear, teddy bear,

jump up high!

Teddy bear, teddy bear,

touch the sky!

 TOT TIME Challenge your toddler to pretend to be the teddy bear by turning around, touching the ground, and jumping up high on cue.

Color the teddy bear 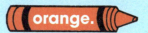 orange.

 TOT TIME Invite your toddler to use an actual teddy bear to act out the rhyme as you read it.

Little Red Wagon

Bumping up and down

in a little red wagon.

Bumping up and down

in a little red wagon.

Up, down, all around—

won't you be my buddy?

 Sit your toddler on your lap, bumping him or her up and down on your knees as you read the rhyme. Share the rhyme again, each time reading it a bit faster.

Color the wagon  red.

TOT TIME
If you have a wagon, treat your toddler to a ride. If you don't, use a big box to make a pretend wagon.

Here Is a Bunny

Here is a bunny

with ears so funny

and fur of fuzzy brown.

When a noise he hears,

he pricks his ears.

And jumps in a hole

in the ground!

 On *ears so funny*, hold two fingers above your head like bunny ears. On *when a noise he hears*, cup a hand to your ear. On *jumps in a hole*, jump up, then down on the ground. Challenge your toddler to do the same.

Color the bunny brown.

TOT TIME Invite your toddler to pretend he or she is a bunny and hop around inside or outside.

Rub-a-Dub-Dub

Rub-a-dub-dub,

three pals in a tub.

And who do you

think they be?

A dog, a cat, and a kid

named _____.

toddler's name

All of them float

on the sea!

TOT TIME Change the animals in the fifth line to new creatures, such as *a frog, a fairy, and a kid named Alyssa*. Then, share the new version with your toddler.

Help your toddler color the paper-doll shape to resemble him- or herself.

 TOT TIME Talk about—and demonstrate!—things that can float on water, such as a toy boat or a rubber ducky.

Jack-in-the-Box

Jack-in-the-box,

jack-in-the-box

sits so still.

Will you pop out?

Yes, I will!

 TOT TIME Invite your child to pretend to be a jack-in-the-box by crouching down low on *sits so still*, then springing up high on *Yes, I will!*

Color the box  pink.

 TOT TIME If you have a jack-in-the-box, share it with your toddler. If not, watch an online video of one.

Zoom, Zoom, Zoom!

Zoom, zoom, zoom!

We're going to the moon.

If you want to take a trip,

climb aboard my rocket ship.

Zoom, zoom, zoom!

We're going to the moon.

5, 4, 3, 2, 1—

Blast off!

 TOT TIME Make a rocket ship out of a toilet-paper tube, inviting your toddler to "blast off" at the end of the rhyme.

Color the rocket ship  green.

Hey, Diddle, Diddle

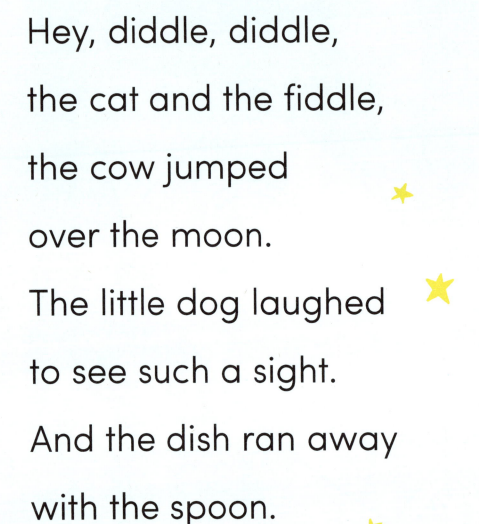

Hey, diddle, diddle,

the cat and the fiddle,

the cow jumped

over the moon.

The little dog laughed

to see such a sight.

And the dish ran away

with the spoon.

TOT TIME Act out the rhyme with items you have in your home, such as a toy (or stuffed) cat, cow, and dog and/or a plastic dish and spoon.

Color the moon  yellow.

TOT TIME Use this picture to make up a simple story about one or all of the characters shown.

Little Boy Blue

Little boy blue,

come blow your horn.

The sheep's in the meadow,

the cow's in the corn.

But where is the boy

who looks after the sheep?

He's under a haystack,

fast asleep.

 TOT TIME On the last two lines of the rhyme, rest your head on your hands, pretend to fall asleep, and say ZZZZZZZZZ. Invite your toddler to do the same.

Color the little boy  blue.

 TOT TIME   Why do children take naps? Talk about it with your toddler.

Little Miss Muffet

Little Miss Muffet

sat on a tuffet,

eating her curds and whey.

Along came a spider,

who sat down beside her

and frightened

Miss Muffet away.

 TOT TIME Change *Little Miss Muffet* to someone else—dad, grandma, your dog, a prince—then reread the revised rhyme. (NOTE: If changing to a male, you will also have to change each *her* to *him*.)

Color the spider black.

Spiders are amazing! Show your toddler an online video of one spinning a web.

Roses Are Red

Roses are red.

Violets are blue.

Sugar is sweet

and so are you!

Elephants are big.

Butterflies are not.

I love _____
toddler's name

a lot, lot, lot!

 TOT TIME Replace *roses* and *violets* with other things that are red and blue, such as *apples* and *whales*. Replace *elephants* and *butterflies* with other things that are big and small, such as *dinosaurs* and *fairies*.

Trace and color the hearts  pink.

TOT TIME Talk to your toddler about other things that are red and blue and big and small.

MORE TRACING

SUPPLIES: crayons or washable markers

The pages in this section will continue to develop your toddler's tracing ability. Simply read the directions aloud, then invite him or her to trace the circles, hexagons, hearts, and more.

These shape activities here are a bit more challenging than in the first section, so feel free to guide your child's hand. To reinforce learning, draw shapes in a sandbox, inviting your child to use his or her fingers to copy them.

Follow up your child's tracing sessions with the TOT TIME activities at the bottom of the page. These fun prompts will help build early speaking and listening skills.

Trace the falling rain.

TOT TIME Does your child like rainy days? Talk about it.

Trace the swirl on the lion's lollipop.

 TOT TIME This lion loves lollipops. What is your child's favorite treat?

Trace the rabbit's heart-shaped balloons.

 TOT TIME   A heart means *love*. What are some things your child loves?

Trace the kites in the sky.

TOT TIME

Kites fly in the sky. What else flies in the sky?

Trace the stars in the sky.

 TOT TIME We see stars at night. What else do we see in the night sky?

Trace the little ladybugs.

Ladybugs are small. Talk about other things that are small.

Trace the BIG dinosaur.

 TOT TIME A dinosaur is BIG! Talk about other things that are BIG.

Trace the panda's pizza.

 TOT TIME Pizza is for sharing. What else can be shared?

MORE COLORING

SUPPLIES: crayons or washable markers

The pages in this section will continue to help your toddler recognize and name colors. Simply read the directions aloud, then invite him or her to color each item.

To extend learning, take an indoor or outdoor walk with your child, looking for things that are red, blue, yellow, green, orange, purple, pink, brown, black, or white. What color do you see the most?

Follow up your child's coloring sessions with the TOT TIME activities at the bottom of the page. These fun prompts will help build early speaking and listening skills.

Color the stop sign red.

STOP

 TOT TIME Play a game of "Go and Stop." When you say "Go," your child goes; when you say "Stop," your child stops.

Color the flower  blue.

TOT TIME Talk about flowers and their special parts, including petals, stems, and leaves.

Color the taxi yellow.

 TOT TIME Pretend you're climbing in a taxi with your child. Where does he/she want to go today?

Color the tree **green.**

 TOT TIME Go on a walk and look at two trees. How are they alike and different?

Color the pumpkin orange.

 TOT TIME We see pumpkins in fall. What other things do we see in fall?

176

Color the grapes purple.

 TOT TIME Grapes are a yummy fruit. Talk about other fruits.

Color the cake pink.

 TOT TIME It's Bunny's birthday! How old is she?
HINT: Count the candles to find out.

Color the cookie  brown.

Bake a batch of cookies with your child. Who can you share them with?

Color the cat  black.

 TOT TIME **What sounds do cats make?** *Meow*, *purr*, and *mew* with your child.

Color the snowman  white.

TOT TIME Talk about snow. Is there snow where you live?
Is snow hot or cold?

181

Color the rainbow

 TOT TIME Point to each color in the rainbow, inviting your child to say its name.

MORE DRAWING

SUPPLIES: crayons or washable markers

The pages in this section will continue to help your toddler develop early drawing skills. Simply read the directions aloud, then invite him or her to draw legs on a creepy-crawly, apples on a tree, and more.

Since toddlers are just learning how to use crayons or markers, their drawings will likely be less than perfect. Don't worry! The primary goal is to build confidence and promote a love of learning.

Follow up your child's drawing sessions with the TOT TIME activities at the bottom of the page. These fun prompts will help build early speaking and listening skills.

Draw more legs on the creepy-crawly.

 TOT TIME Does this creepy-crawly have a few legs or a lot of legs? Talk about it.

Draw more apples on the tree.

 Apples grow on trees. Talk about other things that grow on trees.

Draw more rain falling from the cloud.

 TOT TIME What are some fun things to do on a rainy day? Talk about it.

Draw more snow falling from the cloud.

Does it snow where you live? Talk about it.

Draw more zigzags on the cat's t-shirt.

 TOT TIME This cat loves her T-shirt! What is your child's favorite thing to wear?

Draw more dots on the dog's T-shirt.

TOT TIME This T-shirt has dots. Can you spot more things in your home that have dots?

Draw a surprised face and a mad face.

 TOT TIME What makes your child surprised and mad? Talk about it.

Draw more hats on the clowns.

 TOT TIME Clowns are funny. What else makes your child giggle?

191

MORE CUTTING & PASTING

SUPPLIES: safety scissors and nontoxic glue stick

The pages in this section provide more experience cutting and pasting, which will build important fine motor skills. Simply read the directions aloud, then work together to cut and paste the shapes to create surprise pictures.
NOTE: Always supervise children when using scissors.

As in the previous section, if your child is too young to cut out a shape effectively, feel free to guide his or her hand when using the safety scissors. Or, do the cutting yourself. The gluing, too, can be done with or without your help. Cutting and pasting are skills that take practice, so be patient and focus on having a good time.

Follow up your child's cutting-and-pasting sessions with the TOT TIME activities at the bottom of the page. These fun prompts will help build early speaking and listening skills.

Cut out the rhombus shape and paste it on page 195.

Paste the rhombus shape here. What do you see?

TOT TIME This tiger is flying a kite in the sky. What other toys can you play with outside?

There are three rhombus shapes in this picture. Can your child find them?

 TOT TIME Make up a silly story about this monkey.

Cut out the heart shape and paste it on page 199.

Paste the heart shape here. What do you see?

 TOT TIME How many pandas on are this page? How many balloons? Count them together.

Point to the heart-shaped candy in the box. What other shapes do you see?

Point to each shape in the box and say its name.

Cut out the crescent shape and paste it on page 203.

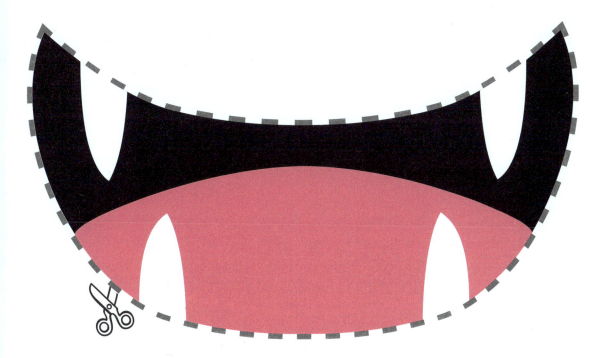

Paste the crescent shape here. What do you see?

TOT TIME — This monster is smiling. What makes your child smile?

203

Find the crescent shape in the picture. What is it?

TOT TIME What other things do you see in this night picture? Talk about it.

Cut out the star shape and paste it on page 207.

Paste the star shape here. What do you see?

What other animals live in the ocean? Talk about it.

How many stars do you see in the night sky? Count them together.

TOT TIME What does your child like to do at night? Talk about it.

Cut out the hexagon shape and paste it on page 211.

Paste the hexagon shape here. What do you see?

TOT TIME Spiders can spin webs. What else can they do? Talk about it.

Find the hexagon shapes on the hive.

TOT TIME Bees live in hives. Talk about other animals homes.

MORE MATCHING

SUPPLIES: crayons or washable markers

The pages here are designed to provide your toddler with slightly more challenging matching activities than in the first section. Simply read the directions, then invite him or her to draw lines to match the like items. NOTE: A dashed line is provided for the first match.

To reinforce learning, place three sets of like objects on a table—such as two apples, two oranges, two bananas—challenging your child to make real-life matches.

Follow up your child's matching sessions with the TOT TIME activities at the bottom of the page. These fun prompts will help build early speaking and listening skills.

Draw lines to match the clothes.

Draw lines to match the vegetables.

 TOT TIME Challenge your child to name these vegetables. Can he/she think of more?

Draw lines to match the sea creatures.

Challenge your child to name these sea creatures.
Can he/she think of more?

Draw lines to match the insects.

TOT TIME

Challenge your child to name these insects.
Can he/she think of more?

Draw lines to match these things that grow.

TOT TIME Challenge your child to name these things that grow. Can he/she think of more?

Draw lines to match the foods.

 Challenge your child to name these foods.
Can he/she think of more?

Draw lines to match the things in the day sky.

 Challenge your child to name these things in the day sky. Can he/she think of more?

Draw lines to match these things in the night sky.

 - - - - - - - - - - -

 TOT TIME Challenge your child to name these things in the night sky. Can he/she think of more?

221

MORE SORTING

SUPPLIES: safety scissors, nontoxic glue stick

The pages in this section provide toddlers with more experience sorting as well as cutting and pasting. Simply read the directions, then invite your child to cut out the two items at the bottom of the page and paste each in the correct group. NOTE: Always supervise children when using scissors.

If your toddler is too young to cut effectively, feel free to guide his or her hand when using the safety scissors. The gluing, too, can be done with or without your help. Cutting and pasting are skills that take time and practice, so be patient and focus on fun.

Follow up your child's sorting sessions with the TOT TIME activities at the bottom of the page. These instant prompts will help build early speaking and listening skills.

Cut out the letter and number at the bottom of the page. Then, paste each in the right group.

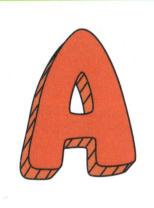 

TOT TIME Find items in your home that begin with A, B, and C. Then, count items in groups of three.

Point to each letter as you sing the alphabet song.

A B C D E F

G H I J K

L M N O P

Q R S T U

V W X Y Z

Cut out the red and blue items at the bottom of the page. Then, paste each in the right group.

TOT TIME Point out items in your home or neighborhood that are red and blue.

Point to each T-shirt, challenging your toddler to tell you if it is red or blue.

Cut out the yellow and green items at the bottom of the page. Then, paste each in the right group.

TOT TIME

Point out items in your home or neighborhood that are yellow and green.

Point to each balloon, challenging your toddler to tell you if it is yellow or green.

Cut out the orange and purple items at the bottom of the page. Then, paste each in the right group.

TOT TIME

Point out items in your home or neighborhood that are orange and purple.

Point to each party hat, challenging your toddler to tell you if it is orange or purple.

Cut out the shapes at the bottom of the page.
Then, paste each in the right group.

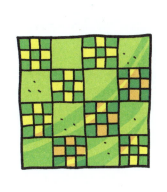

TOT TIME

Point out items in your home or neighborhood that are circles and squares.

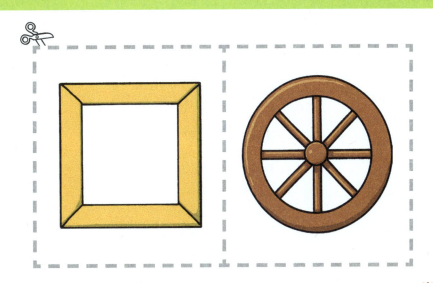

Point to each window, challenging your toddler to tell you if it is a circle or a square.

Cut out the shapes at the bottom of the page. Then, paste each in the right group.

 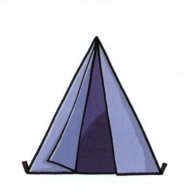

TOT TIME Point out items in your home or neighborhood that are triangles and rectangles.

Point to each shape, challenging your toddler to tell you if it is a triangle or a rectangle.

MORE ALPHABET

SUPPLIES: crayons or washable markers

The pages in this section provide more alphabet experience to help your toddler identify the letters *A* to *Z*. Simply read the directions aloud, then invite him or her to trace the featured letter, such as *A*, and color the three items that begin with it.

To reinforce learning, point to each of the items that begin with the featured letter—such as *ant, apple,* and *alligator.* Read the name of each slowly and clearly several times, inviting your child to chime in with you.

Follow up your child's alphabet sessions with the TOT TIME activities at the bottom of the page. These fun prompts will help build early speaking and listening skills.

Trace the letter. Then color the things that begin with A.

ant

alligator

apple

TOT TIME Invite your child to point to each picture and say its name with or without your help.

Trace the letter. Then color the things that begin with B.

balloon

bear

bus

 TOT TIME Invite your child to point to each picture and say its name with or without your help.

Trace the letter. Then color the things that begin with C.

car

cake

cat

TOT TIME Invite your child to point to each picture and say its name with or without your help.

238

Trace the letter. Then color the things that begin with D.

dog

duck

donut

Trace the letter. Then color the things that begin with E.

egg

elephant

Earth

 TOT TIME Invite your child to point to each picture and say its name with or without your help.

240

Trace the letter. Then color the things that begin with F.

fish

fox

fire

TOT TIME Invite your child to point to each picture and say its name with or without your help.

Trace the letter. Then color the things that begin with G.

ghost

gorilla

gift

TOT TIME

Invite your child to point to each picture and say its name with or without your help.

Trace the letter. Then color the things that begin with H.

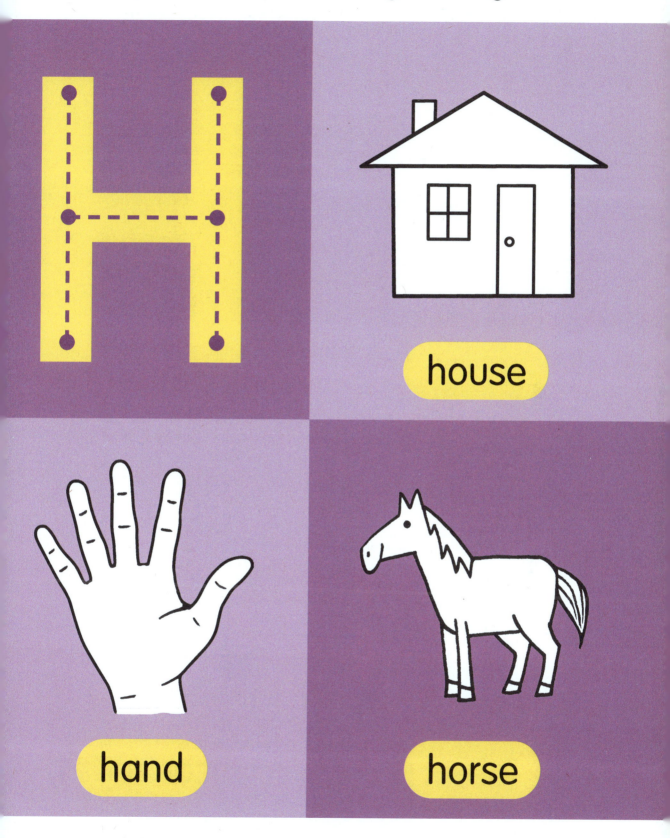

house

hand

horse

 Invite your child to point to each picture and say its name with or without your help.

Trace the letter. Then color the things that begin with I.

iguana

insect

ice cream

TOT TIME Invite your child to point to each picture and say its name with or without your help.

Trace the letter. Then color the things that begin with J.

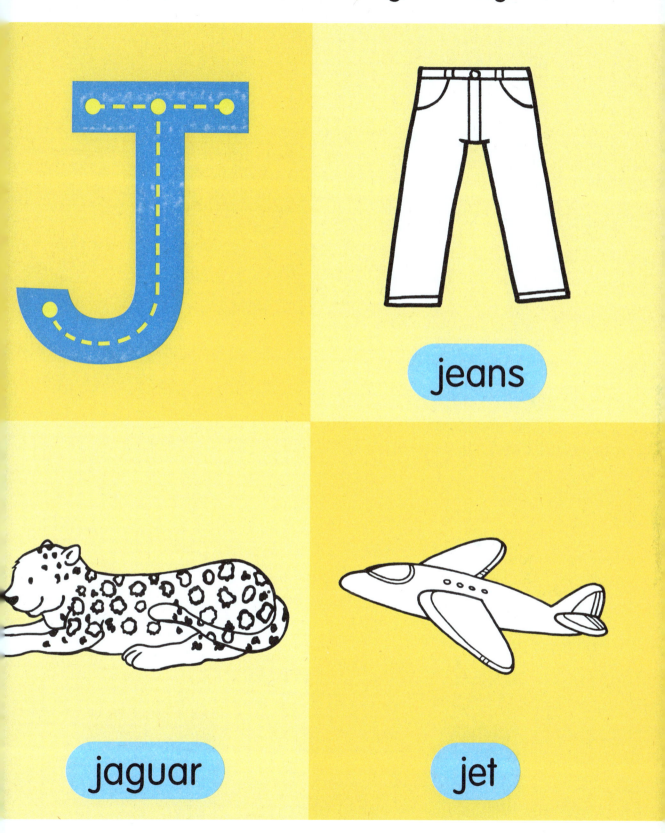

jeans

jaguar

jet

Trace the letter. Then color the things that begin with K.

kangaroo

kite

key

TOT TIME Invite your child to point to each picture and say its name with or without your help.

Trace the letter. Then color the things that begin with L.

lamp

lion

lollipop

247

Trace the letter. Then color the things that begin with M.

mouse

moon

mermaid

Invite your child to point to each picture and say its name with or without your help.

Trace the letter. Then color the things that begin with N.

nest

noodles

nose

Invite your child to point to each picture and say its name with or without your help.

Trace the letter. Then color the things that begin with O.

owl

octopus

orange

 TOT TIME Invite your child to point to each picture and say its name with or without your help.

Trace the letter. Then color the things that begin with P.

penguin

pig

pizza

251

Trace the letter. Then color the things that begin with Q.

queen

quail

quilt

 TOT TIME Invite your child to point to each picture and say its name with or without your help.

Trace the letter. Then color the things that begin with R.

rabbit

rainbow

robot

TOT TIME Invite your child to point to each picture and say its name with or without your help.

253

Trace the letter. Then color the things that begin with S.

sun

seal

socks

TOT TIME
Invite your child to point to each picture and say its name with or without your help.

254

Trace the letter. Then color the things that begin with T.

tiger

taco

tent

Invite your child to point to each picture and say its name with or without your help.

Trace the letter. Then color the things that begin with U.

urchin

underwear

umbrella

 TOT TIME Invite your child to point to each picture and say its name with or without your help.

Trace the letter. Then color the things that begin with V.

violin

velociraptor

van

Trace the letter. Then color the things that begin with W.

wheel

whale

watermelon

TOT TIME Invite your child to point to each picture and say its name with or without your help.

Trace the letter. Then color the things that have an X.

x-ray fish

mix

box

 TOT TIME Invite your child to point to each picture and say its name with or without your help.

259

Trace the letter. Then color the things that begin with Y.

yo-yo

yak

yarn

TOT TIME Invite your child to point to each picture and say its name with or without your help.

Trace the letter. Then color the things that begin with Z.

zebra

zipper

zoo

Color the silly Alphabet Bug.

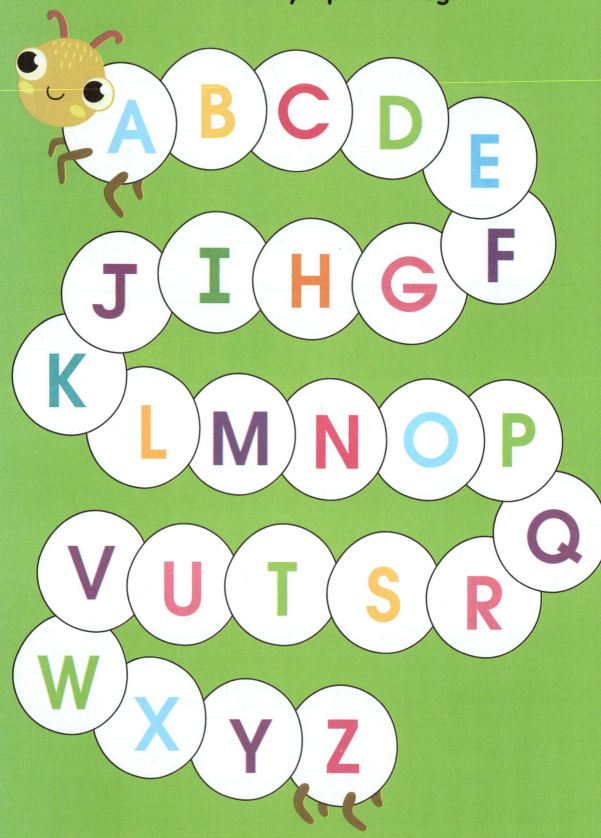

TOT TIME Invite your child to point to each letter and say its name with or without your help.

MORE NUMBERS

SUPPLIES: crayons or washable markers

The pages in this section will continue to develop your toddler's ability to recognize and name the numbers 1 through 10. Simply read the directions aloud, then invite him or her to trace the featured number, such as 2, and color the corresponding picture: *two mittens.*

To reinforce early number sense, work with your child to count the items on each page, such as *two mittens, three monkeys,* or *four robots.*

Follow up your child's number sessions with the TOT TIME activities at the bottom of the page. These fun prompts will help build early speaking and listening skills.

Trace the number. Then color the one dragon.

TOT TIME Invite your child to point to and count the dragon with or without your help.

Trace the number. Then color the two mittens.

TOT TIME Invite your child to point to and count the mittens with or without your help

Trace the number. Then color the three monkeys.

TOT TIME Invite your child to point to and count the monkeys with or without your help.

Trace the number. Then color the four robots.

TOT TIME Invite your child to point to and count the robots with or without your help.

Trace the number. Then color the five jeeps.

Trace the number. Then color the six monsters.

TOT TIME Invite your child to point to and count the monsters with or without your help.

269

Trace the number. Then color the seven ducklings.

 TOT TIME Invite your child to point to and count the ducklings with or without your help.

Trace the number. Then color the eight bumblebees.

TOT TIME Invite your child to point to and count the bumblebees with or without your help.

271

Trace the number. Then color the nine butterflies.

TOT TIME Invite your child to point to and count the butterflies with or without your help.

Trace the number. Then color the ten lollipops.

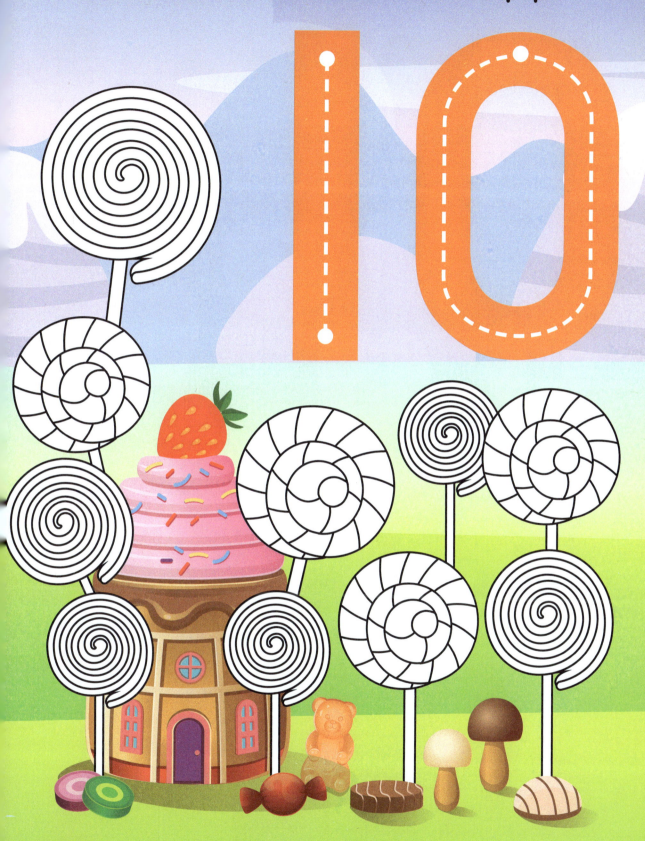

TOT TIME Invite your child to point to and count the lollipops with or without your help.

Color the apples on the apple tree.

TOT TIME Invite your child to point to and count the apples with or without your help.

MORE SHAPES

SUPPLIES: crayons or washable markers

The pages in this section will provide your toddler with additional experience tracing and recognizing their favorite shapes. Simply read the directions aloud, then invite him or her to trace around the shapes.

To maximize learning, point to each pictured item, such as the gift box, and announce its shape: square. Then, challenge your child to walk about the room and find something else that is square.

Follow up your child's shape sessions with the TOT TIME activities at the bottom of the page. These fun prompts will help build early speaking and listening skills.

Trace the triangle shapes.

 TOT TIME Talk about other things that are a triangle shape.

Trace the square shapes.

Talk about other things that are a square shape.

Trace the circle shapes.

 TOT TIME **Talk about other things that are a circle shape.**

Trace the rectangle shapes.

 Talk about other things that are a rectangular shape.

Trace the oval shapes.

TOT TIME Talk about other things that are an oval shape.

Trace the rhombus shapes.

Trace the star shapes.

 TOT TIME   **Talk about other things that are a star shape.**

Trace the heart shapes.

LOVE YOU

CUTIE

COOL KID

BIG HUG

YOU ROCK

XOXO

 TOT TIME Talk about other things that are a heart shape.

Trace and review the shapes.

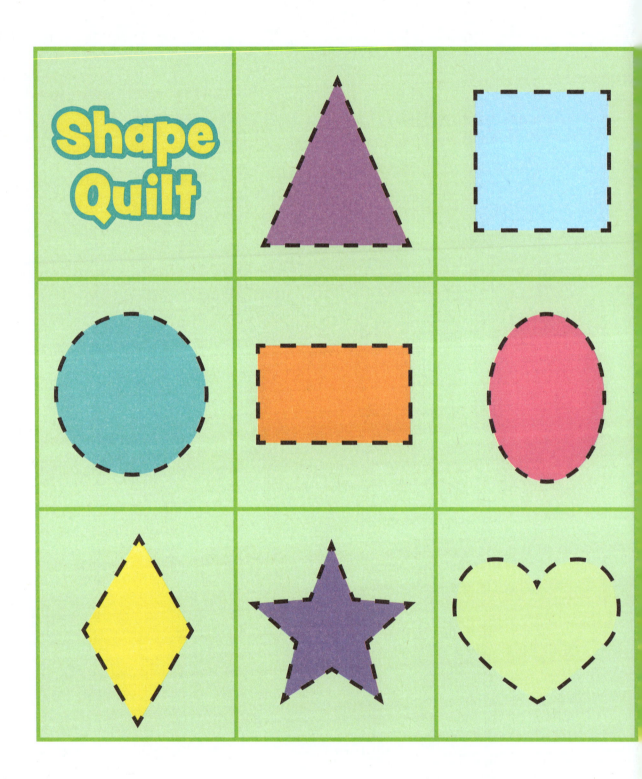

Shape Quilt

 TOT TIME Invite your child to point to each shape and name it with or without your help.

EASY SONGS

SUPPLIES: crayons or washable markers

Like nursery rhymes, classic songs are enjoyable and packed with learning. Not only do these "sticky" tunes boost speaking and vocabulary skills, they also set the stage for reading success because they help toddlers understand how words and language work.

Sing each song slowly, clearly, and with verve—encouraging your toddler to join in. There is no such thing as singing a song too many times. TIP: If you are unfamiliar with a particular song, find it online and give it a listen. You'll pick up the tune in no time.

Don't forget to try the TOT TIME idea at the bottom of the page. These simple kinesthetic activities give kids the opportunity to hop, skip, dance, and do fingerplays. Last but not least, extend learning with each song's companion page, which provide added opportunities to think, write, and draw.

Sing the song with your toddler.

Pop Goes the Weasel

Round and round

the mulberry bush,

the monkey chased

the weasel.

The monkey thought

'twas all in fun—

POP goes the weasel.

 As you sing, walk in a circle—or around a Hula-Hoop™— with your toddler. On *POP goes the weasel*, crouch down low, then jump up high.

Color the berries on the bush   **red.**

 TOT TIME Reread the rhyme, substituting two other animals for *monkey* and *weasel*, such as *kitty* and *bunny*. Or act it out with stuffed animals.

287

The Itsy Bitsy Spider

The itsy bitsy spider

crawled up the water spout.

Down came the rain,

and washed the spider out.

Out came the sun,

and dried up all the rain,

and the itsy bitsy spider

went up the spout again.

 On *crawled up the water spout,* run your fingers up your toddler's arm. On *washed the spider out,* run your fingers down his/her arm. On *out came the sun,* form a sun with your hands. On *went up the spout again,* run your fingers up your toddler's arm to his/her shoulder, then give a thumbs-up.

Color the spider  green.

TOT TIME Read an easy nonfiction book about spiders to your toddler.

Sing the song with your toddler.

Twinkle, Twinkle, Little Star

Twinkle, twinkle, little star,

how I wonder what you are!

Up above the world so high,

like a diamond in the sky.

Twinkle, twinkle, little star,

how I wonder what you are!

TOT TIME

On *Twinkle, twinkle little star*, open and close your hands like twinkling stars. On *how I wonder*, point to your head as if you're thinking. On *up above the world*, reach skyward. On *like a diamond*, form a diamond shape with your two hands. Invite your toddler to copy your movements.

Trace the stars and color them ((yellow. (((

TOT TIME When it gets dark, look at the stars and talk about them with your toddler.

The Ants Go Marching

The ants go marching

one by one, hurrah, hurrah!

The ants go marching

one by one, hurrah, hurrah!

The ants go marching

one by one, the little one stops

to suck his thumb.

And they all go marching

down to the ground

to get out of the rain.

As you sing, invite your toddler to pretend to be a marching ant.

Color the ants  brown.

TOT TIME Ants are amazing! Share an easy nonfiction book about them with your toddler.

The Wheels on the Bus

The wheels on the bus

go round and round,

round and round,

round and round.

The wheels on

the bus go round and round—

all through the town.

 Invite your toddler to pretend to be a bus and go "all through the town."

Color the school bus

 TOT TIME Talk to your child about other vehicles with wheels that go round and round, such as bikes, cars, and trucks.

Row, Row, Row Your Boat

Row, row, row your boat,

gently down the stream.

Merrily, merrily,

merrily, merrily—

life is but a dream.

 Give your toddler two paper-towel tubes to use as oars, inviting him/her to "row" as you sing.

Trace the waves on the ocean.

TOT TIME Talk to your toddler about boats. Then, read a fiction or nonfiction book about them!

297

London Bridge

London Bridge is falling down,

falling down,

falling down.

London Bridge is falling down—

my fair lady.

Build it up with sticks and stones,

sticks and stones,

sticks and stones—

my fair lady.

On *London Bridge is falling down*, flutter your fingers downward to suggest falling. On *Build it up with sticks and stones*, place a fist on top of a fist to suggest building. Invite your toddler to copy you.

TOT TIME

Help fix the bridge by putting a  on each of its broken parts.

It's Raining, It's Pouring

It's raining, it's pouring,

the old man is snoring.

He went to bed and

bumped his head

and dreamt of cats

'til the morning.

 TOT TIME Change *cats* to another animal or item—such as *dogs* or *cake*—then sing the poem again.

Color the cats  black and orange.

I'm a Little Teapot

I'm a little teapot,

short and stout.

Here is my handle,

here is my spout.

When I get all steamed up,

hear me shout.

Just tip me over,

and pour me out!

TOT TIME On *Here is my handle*, put your left hand on your hip. On *here is my spout*, stick out your right arm. On *tip me over and pour me out*, bend your body to the right as if pouring out tea. Invite your toddler to do the same.

Color the teapot green.

TOT TIME Have a tea party with your toddler and his/her stuffed animals.

Six Little Ducks

Six little ducks went to play—

wibble wobble, wibble wobble

to and fro.

But the one little duck

with the feather on his back,

he led the others with a

quack, quack, quack.

Quack, quack, quack.

Quack, quack, quack.

 As you sing, invite your toddler to pretend to be a duck by waddling, flapping his/her arms, and quacking.

Count the ducks and color them yellow.

TOT TIME Challenge your toddler to find "the one little duck with the feather on his back." Then, go to a park and feed some ducks!

Mary Had a Little Lamb

Mary had a little lamb,

little lamb, little lamb.

Mary had a little lamb,

its fleece was white as snow.

And everywhere that Mary went,

Mary went, Mary went.

Everywhere that Mary went,

the lamb was sure to go.

TOT TIME Change *Mary* to the name of your toddler. Then, sing it again!

Trace the lamb's fur, then color it white.

TOT TIME Invite your toddler to pretend to be a lamb and say "Baaaah!"

If You're Happy and You Know It

If you're happy and you know it,

clap your hands. (CLAP, CLAP.)

If you're happy and you know it,

clap your hands. (CLAP, CLAP.)

If you're happy and you know it,

then your face will surely show it.

If you're happy and you know it,

clap your hands. (CLAP, CLAP.)

Each time *clap your hands* is sung, invite your toddler to clap his/her hands twice. On *then your face will surely show it*, invite him/her to smile broadly.

Trace the smiles on the happy faces.

 TOT TIME Count the happy faces with your toddler. Then, talk about things that make him/her happy.

309

Old MacDonald

Old MacDonald had a farm,

E-I-E-I-O.

And on his farm, he had a cow,

E-I-E-I-O.

With a MOO, MOO here

and a MOO, MOO there.

Here a MOO, there a MOO,

everywhere a MOO, MOO!

Old MacDonald had a farm,

E-I-E-I-O.

TOT TIME Sing the song again, but replace "cow" and "MOO" with a new animal and sound; for example: *And on his farm he had a* <u>horse</u>*, E-I-E-I-O. With a "NEIGH, NEIGH" here and a "NEIGH, NEIGH" there.*

Trace the cow's spots and color them black.

Rock-a-Bye Baby

Rock-a-bye, baby

in the treetop.

When the wind blows,

the cradle will rock.

When the bough breaks

the cradle will fall.

And Mommy will catch you—

cradle and all.

TOT TIME As you sing, rock your toddler on your lap. Or invite your toddler to rock a doll or stuffed animal.
NOTE: *Mommy* can be changed to *Daddy*, *Auntie*, etc.

Trace the leaves on the tree and color them 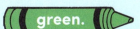 green.

Share baby pictures with your toddler. Discuss how he/she has changed and learned new things.

BONUS SECTION

SUPPLIES: crayons or washable markers

Congratulations! Your child has almost completed the *Jumbo Book of Toddler Fun*! To celebrate, you'll find BONUS ACTIVITIES in the following section. These activities focus on what makes your incredible toddler totally unique.

Read the directions aloud. Then work together to complete the pages related to age, name, and favorite activities.

We've also included a fun fill-in chant AND a special certificate to mark the completion of this workbook. Be sure to fill it out and present it to your child along with cheers and a big round of applause. May it be the first of many stepping stones on a long and joyful path of learning.

MY NAME IS

_____

Child's name

Invite your child to find and circle the letter his/her name begins with.

A B C D E F G H I
J K L M N O P Q
R S T U V W X Y Z

A fun fact about my name is...

_____

_____

Write a fact about your child's name here.

Fill in your child's age, inviting him/her to circle that number and color in the candles to match it.

MY AGE IS

Write child's age

Age (Circle one)

1 2 3 4 5

My wish is...

_____

_____

Write your child's wish here.

MY HAND IS SMALL, BUT MIGHTY!

Trace your child's handprint, inviting him or her to color it.

Three AWESOME things I can do are...

 _____

 _____

 _____

Above write three things your child can do.

Work with your child to write his or her favorite things in the boxes.

_____ **'S**

child's name

 FAVORITES

Color	Animal	Food
Book	Toy	Song
Game	Stuffed Animal	Pal
Place	Activity	Thing to Say

CONGRATULATIONS TO

child's name

This incredible little learner has completed the *Jumbo Book of Toddler Fun.*

Hip, hip, hooray!